DO COWS HAVE TWO STOMACHS?

And Other FAQs About Animals

By Therese M. Shea

 Gareth Stevens
PUBLISHING

Please visit our website, www.garethstevens.com. For a free color catalog of all our high-quality books, call toll free 1-800-542-2595 or fax 1-877-542-2596.

Cataloging-in-Publication Data

Names: Shea, Therese M.
Title: Do cows have two stomachs? / Therese M. Shea.
Description: New York : Gareth Stevens Publishing, 2017. | Series: Q & A: life's mysteries solved!| Includes index.
Identifiers: ISBN 9781482449617 (pbk.) | ISBN 9781482447781 (library bound) | ISBN 9781482447774 (6 pack)
Subjects: LCSH: Animals–Miscellanea–Juvenile literature. | Animals–Juvenile literature.
Classification: LCC QL49.S44 2017 | DDC 590–dc23

Published in 2017 by
Gareth Stevens Publishing
111 East 14th Street, Suite 349
New York, NY 10003

Copyright © 2017 Gareth Stevens Publishing

Designer: Andrea Davison-Bartolotta
Editor: Kristen Nelson

Photo credits: Cover, p. 1 (cow) rclassenlayouts/iStock/Thinkstock; cover, p. 1 (barn) owatta/Shutterstock.com; pp. 4, 6, 8, 11, 13, 14, 16, 19, 20, 22, 25, 27 (notebook) BeatWalk/Shutterstock.com; p. 4 (scientist) Daniela Barreto/Shutterstock.com; p. 5 (monkey) l i g h t p o e t/Shutterstock.com; p. 5 (Komodo dragon) Richard Susanto/Shutterstock.com; p. 5 (whale) Seb c'est bien/Shutterstock.com; p. 5 (anteater) Ondrej Prosicky/Shutterstock.com; p. 5 (slug) Frances van der Merwe/Shutterstock.com; p. 5 (mouse) Rudmer Zwerver/Shutterstock.com; p. 5 (hummingbird) Glass and Nature/Shutterstock.com; p. 6 (left) Auscape/Universal Images Group/Getty Images; p. 6 (right) The Asahi Shimbun/Getty Images; p. 7 Robert Proctor/Shutterstock.com; p. 8 (inset) Janelle Lugge/Shutterstock.com; p. 8 (main) worldswildlifewonders/Shutterstock.com; p. 9 Shane Gross/Shutterstock.com; p. 10 (tarsier) PhotoBarmaley/Shutterstock.com; p. 10 (seal) David Doubilet/Getty Images; p. 10 (bighorn sheep) gnohz/Shutterstock.com; p. 10 (whale) Metaphoricalplatypus/Wikimedia Commons; p. 10 (bear) critterbiz/Shutterstock.com; p. 10 (pangolin) 2630ben/Shutterstock.com; p. 10 (flying lemur) Butterfly Hunter/Shutterstock.com; p. 11 JoeGough/iStock/Thinkstock; p. 12 (feather) Potapov Alexander/Shutterstock.com; p. 12 (bat) Ivan Kuzmin/Shutterstock.com; p. 13 (main) Regien Passen/Shutterstock.com; p. 13 (inset) AuntSpray/Shutterstock.com; p. 14 fieldwork/Shutterstock.com; p. 15 (cassowary) hin255/Shutterstock.com; p. 15 (kiwi) John Carnemolla/Shutterstock.com; p. 15 (emu) S. Cooper Digital/Shutterstock.com; p. 15 (rhea) Steve Meese/Shutterstock.com; p. 15 (ostriches) Michel Piccaya/Shutterstock.com; p. 16 (chameleon) Robert Eastman/Shutterstock.com; p. 16 (frog) Dirk Ercken/Shutterstock.com; p. 16 (turtle) Willyam Bradberry/Shutterstock.com; p. 16 (salamander) Matt Jeppson/Shutterstock.com; p. 17 Audrey Snider-Bell/Shutterstock.com; p. 18 (toad) Jarkko Jokelainen/Shutterstock.com; p. 18 (crocodile) defpicture/Shutterstock.com; p. 18 (turtle) Svetlana Foote/Shutterstock.com; p. 19 (main) Getty Images News/Getty Images; p. 19 (doodle) Tidarat Tiernjai/Shutterstock.com; p. 20 Wolfgang Zwanzger/Shutterstock.com; p. 21 (bottom) Krzysztof Odziomek/Shutterstock.com; p. 21 (top) Dobermaraner/Shutterstock.com; p. 22 twospeeds/Shutterstock.com; p. 23 Daniel Huebner/Shutterstock.com; p. 24 (scorpion) EcoPrint/Shutterstock.com; p. 24 (clam) Marco Tomasini/Shutterstock.com; p. 24 (spider) jdm.foto/Shutterstock.com; p. 24 (bee) boyphare/Shutterstock.com; p. 24 (worm) Maryna Pleshkun/Shutterstock.com; p. 24 (crab) aodaodaodaod/Shutterstock.com; p. 24 (butterfly) Onrej Prosicky/Shutterstock.com; p. 24 (crayfish) Puripat/Shutterstock.com; p. 25 Lightboxx/Shutterstock.com; p. 26 Joost van Uffelen/Shutterstock.com; p. 27 (top) Chatchai Somwat/Shutterstock.com; p. 27 (bottom) Nattawat Kaewjirasit/Shutterstock.com; p. 28 (starfish) Kletr/Shutterstock.com; p. 28 (aardvark) Eric Isselee/Shutterstock.com; p. 28 (solenodon) Seb az86556/Wikimedia Commons; p. 29 (frogmouth) N A Nazeer/Wikimedia Commons; p. 29 (jawfish) Wild Horizon/Universal Images Group/Getty Images; p. 29 (giant salamander) Michael Stuparyk/Toronto Star/Getty Images.

Printed in the United States of America

CPSIA compliance information: Batch #CS16GS: For further information contact Gareth Stevens, New York, New York at 1-800-542-2595.

Contents

Words in the glossary appear in **bold** type the first time they are used in the text.

ANIMAL KINGDOM

Did you ever try to count all the different **species** of animals you know of? Don't start—it would take you a long, long time. Whether they're hairy, scaly, slimy, two-legged, many-legged, huge, or tiny, Earth is full of the living creatures called animals. In this book, you'll find out many facts about them. Some may seem unbelievable, but they're all true!

Q: How many kinds of animals are there?

A: We don't know! A recent **census** suggests that about 7.77 million species of animals call Earth home. However, we only know of 953,434 species. Why is there a difference between the numbers? Scientists used a special method to **estimate** the higher number because they're certain many animals haven't been discovered yet.

Come Out Wherever You Are!

Scientists think at least two-thirds of all water species have yet to be found! Some of these animals haven't been spotted yet because they're in places we haven't explored much, such as the ocean floor.

giant anteater

squirrel monkey

Komodo dragon

The largest animal on Earth is the blue whale. Most animals seem small compared to it!

slug

hummingbird

mouse

humpback whale

5

Q: What's the difference between plants and animals?

A: Animals can usually move. Even animals that are fixed to one place, such as barnacles, were once able to move. And even when fixed in place, animals can move certain body parts in order to catch something to eat. Plants can't move on their own. Animals also use their senses, though plants have some senses, too!

SEA PEN

MONKEY ORCHID

It's not always easy to tell the difference between a plant and an animal. Shown here are an animal called the sea pen and a plant called the monkey orchid.

Sticking to Home

Barnacles are **crustaceans** that don't look much like plants—or animals! When they're young, though, they look a bit like shrimp. When they get older, they choose a place to settle, such as on rocks, boats, or even shellfish. Then, they use a powerful glue-like matter to stick themselves to the surface. A barnacle then grows into an adult as it stays put for the rest of its life! Its special body parts move to collect food for it.

MARVELOUS MAMMALS

You might know something about mammals. After all, you are one! A mammal is warm-blooded, which means its body temperature stays about the same, no matter the temperature outside its body. It breathes air and has a backbone and hair. Mammal mothers feed milk to their babies. Almost all mammals give birth to live young.

Q: Which mammals don't give birth to live young?

A: Four species of echidnas and one species of platypus lay eggs instead of giving birth to live babies. However, like all mammals do, these creatures take care of their young once they've hatched.

platypus

Echidnas and platypuses still feed their young milk, like all mammals do. Platypuses **release** their milk through their skin, like sweat!

echidna

Mammal with a Mustache!

You can probably think of some mammals that don't have hair. Sometimes, mammals are born with hair and it falls out. That's the case with dolphins. Baby dolphins are born with hair around their **snout**—like a mustache! It helps them find their mother at first, but then falls off about a week later.

HOW Many?

There are more than 5,000 living species of mammals.

insane Adaptations

The animals in the mammal group can look very different. After all, you and a platypus are both mammals, and you don't look much alike! Some of the differences among mammals are interesting **adaptations** that have helped them survive in their **habitats**. Check out the chart to learn more.

MAMMAL		ADAPTATION	WHY
tarsier →		each eye weighs more than its brain	to hunt for food at night
hooded seal		can blow a **sac** out its nose	to draw a mate
bighorn sheep →		**shed** belly and leg fur in summer	to release heat (back fur stays to protect it from sun)
dwarf sperm whale		releases waste (poop!) into water	to confuse predators
American black bear →		can go 100 days without eating	to survive winter months
pangolin		has scales on its sides and back	to act as armor
flying lemur →		skin flap to glide from tree to tree	to keep away from ground predators

Q: Do cows have two stomachs?

A: No, that's a misunderstanding likely believed because cows **digest** in two steps. Some people say a cow has four stomachs. However, others say it has just one stomach with four parts. This is an important adaptation for this mammal. It can take a cow 3 days to digest its food! Each stomach part has a special function in its slow digestive process.

When a cow first swallows its food, it goes to two stomach parts. Then, the cow throws up the food and chews this "cud." When the cow swallows again, the cud goes to two different stomach parts.

BIRDS: WINGED WONDERS

Birds aren't mammals. They're warm-blooded, but they lay eggs. Also unlike mammals, birds have feathers. Birds molt, or lose, their feathers at least once a year to make room for new feathers to grow. Check out the chart to learn more about the different kinds of feathers.

Facts About Feathers

kind	flight feathers	contour feathers	down feathers
where they're found	wings and tail	body	under contour feathers
what they're used for	flight	for show and to cover down feathers	warmth

Bats: Birds or Mammals?

Even though they have wings, bats are mammals. They give birth to live young and are covered with fur, not feathers.

Feathered Dinos

Birds are the only *living* animal with feathers, but at least some dinosaurs had feathers, too!

Q: How do birds lose their feathers and still fly?

A: Birds usually lose the feathers from their wings and tail at different times, so they can still have the ability to fly. However, geese and some other water birds lose them all at once. This means they can't fly for 20 to 40 days while they wait for the new feathers to grow in.

Q: Could penguins ever fly?

A: Scientists think penguins and other flightless birds are **descendants** of birds that could fly. They're not sure why they lost the ability to fly. Some think the birds lived in places where they didn't have to worry about predators, so they didn't have to fly away. Over time, the birds adapted to life on the ground and in the water.

Poor DODO!

The dodo was a flightless bird that lived on the island of Mauritius in the Indian Ocean. Dodos were discovered by people in the 1500s and hunted into **extinction** by 1690.

kiwi

Rheas, emus, ostriches, and cassowaries are related. Penguins and kiwis are not related to them or each other. However, all are flightless birds.

emu

cassowary

rhea

OSTRICH

Q: How do flightless birds protect themselves?

A: Many, such as rheas, emus, and ostriches, have the adaptation of speed. Ostriches, for example, can run up to 45 miles (72 km) per hour. Ostriches also have a deadly 4-inch (10 cm) **talon** on each foot. It's sharp enough to kill a lion!

REMARKABLE REPTILES AND AMAZING AMPHIBIANS

Reptiles and amphibians are sometimes grouped together because they're cold-blooded. That doesn't mean their blood is actually cold. It means they get their body heat from outside their body, such as from sunlight or a warm rock. The animals become more active as they warm up and slow their activities as they cool.

Q: Why do reptiles and amphibians need heat?

A: Some of their bodily functions, such as digestion, don't work unless their body is the right temperature. Imagine going outside after lunch to digest your sandwich! Reptiles and amphibians also need light in order to make **vitamins** to keep their body healthy. People, too, need sunlight in order for their skin to make vitamin D!

salamander

sea turtle

poison dart frog

chameleon

The study of reptiles and amphibians is called herpetology.

NOW I'M TOO HOT!

Reptiles and amphibians also have to protect their bodies from too much heat. That's why they dive into water or move into shade at times on sunny, hot days.

amphibians

live in and around water
(except some toads)

eggs have soft shells, usually laid in water

young are tadpoles that live in water and
have gills, but grow lungs

have thin, moist
skin that helps
them breathe

crocodile

both

cold-blooded

live all over the world,
except Antarctica

have backbones

shed and grow new skin

toad

reptiles

most live on land, but some live in water

some eggs have hard shells, some have soft shells
(some snakes and lizards give birth to live babies)

young look like small adults

have dry, scaly skin

turtle

Q: How can a frog warn of pollution?

A: Frogs—and other amphibians—have **porous** skin. Certain matter in their habitat can pass through their skin. If it's harmful matter, such as some chemicals, it will harm the frog, and that tells us there's dangerous pollution in the area.

Scientists think these frogs didn't grow as they were supposed to because of **pesticides** in their habitat.

FANTASTIC FISH

Like reptiles and amphibians, fish are cold-blooded animals with a backbone. However, they're usually scaly and live in water, breathing through gills and swimming with at least two pairs of fins.

Q: What's the difference between a tadpole and a fish?

A: Both fish and tadpoles live in water and breathe through gills. However, tadpoles aren't covered in scales like most fish are. Also, fish never change their body parts, while the tadpoles of amphibians begin to lose their fin-like parts as they grow legs.

TADPOLES

Ick-what?

Ichthyology (ihk-thee-AH-luh-jee) is the study of fish.

Fish can look remarkably different. The whale shark, shown below, can grow to 59 feet (18 m) long, while many aquarium fish are less than 1 inch (2.5 cm) long.

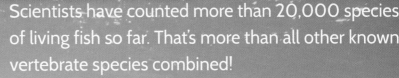

AnD Counting...

Scientists have counted more than 20,000 species of living fish so far. That's more than all other known vertebrate species combined!

Q: Can you teach a fish to do a trick?

A: Yes, you can! Some fish can be taught to swim toward sounds or to spread their fins. In fact, some ichthyologists believe fish are smarter than we might think. A recent study showed fish, even of different species, can work together to find food and trick each other, too!

Q: Are there really fish that can walk?

A: Yes, some fish can walk, but not like other animals do. They don't have legs. Rather, they use their fins and gills to move themselves forward. The movement looks more like a flop than a step. Sometimes the fish do this to travel from one body of water to another. The climbing perch, a native of Asia, has lungs as well as gills and can stay out of water for 6 days!

MUDSKIPPERS

Not All That Swims Is a Fish!

Don't forget there are a lot of other kinds of animals in the water, including mammals such as dolphins and **invertebrates** such as jellyfish.

Q: Are there really flying fish?

A: The estimated 40 species of flying fish don't really fly. However, they swim so fast that—when they leave the water—they can glide through the air with the help of their fins. They probably do this to escape predators.

INTERESTING INVERTEBRATES

All the animals you've read about so far are vertebrates—animals with a backbone. But we can't stop learning about animals there. More than 90 percent of all living animals don't have a backbone! They're called invertebrates, and they're also cold-blooded. Invertebrates usually have a soft body, but can look quite different from each other. They include insects, spiders, crustaceans, worms, and **mollusks**.

INVERTEBRATE INTERROGATION

Y N
☑ ☐ Is it missing a backbone?
☑ ☐ Is it cold-blooded?
☑ ☐ Does it move, or has it ever moved?
☑ ☐ Does it need food from outside its own body?

Q: How do invertebrates protect their soft body?

A: Many invertebrates, such as scorpions, clams, and lobsters, have an outer casing called an exoskeleton. The type of casing depends on the building material. Beetles make a hard matter called chitin. Snails use calcium carbonate for their shell. Other invertebrates have soft bodies without a shell. Some, such as tapeworms, live in other animals' bodies, so they don't need a shell!

All these animals belong to the group called invertebrates. Some have little in common except for their lack of a backbone.

RHINOCEROS BEETLE

25

Q: Are all invertebrates small?

A: No, some are large—scary large! The Amazonian giant centipede can reach 1 foot (30 cm) long. The giant squid's body can be more than 26 feet (8 m) long. The lion's mane jellyfish can grow to be 49 feet (15 m) long!

The lion's mane jellyfish can be many colors. It lives in the cold waters of the Arctic, the northern Pacific, and the northern Atlantic Oceans.

Q: Are all invertebrates gross like worms or annoying like mosquitoes?

A: One animal's "gross" is another's **gourmet** meal! Invertebrates are an important part of many animal food chains. They eat animals and plants and are food for animals, too. Without invertebrates, food chains would become unbalanced, and many plants and animals would suffer—even us!

MILLIPEDE

CENTIPEDE VS. MILLIPEDE

There's a difference between these two many-legged invertebrates that doesn't have to do with their number of legs: Centipedes are carnivores, or meat eaters, while millipedes are herbivores, or plant eaters.

CENTIPEDE

THE ODDEST ANIMAL INFO

Are you ready to read about some truly weird animals? These aren't the only odd facts you'll find. Check out your local zoo, aquarium, or library to learn more!

EERIE INVERTEBRATES

Invertebrates called echinoderms don't have a head.

A species of ribbon worm might be the longest animal on Earth, as long as 197 feet (60 m).

Octopuses have three hearts.

MYSTERIOUS MAMMALS

Solenodons have existed for at least 76 million years and make their own **venom**.

The aardvark's closest relative is the elephant.

BAFFLING BIRDS

The male ribbon-tailed astrapia has tail feathers almost three times as long as its body.

The Sri Lanka frogmouth can make itself look like a tree branch to escape predators.

The California condor can fly 3 miles (4.8 m) without flapping its large wings.

CONFOUNDING FISH

Pacu (nicknamed nutcracker fish) have teeth that look like human teeth.

After a female jawfish lays her eggs, the male jawfish takes them in his mouth and keeps them there until they hatch.

ASTOUNDING AMPHIBIANS AND REPTILES

Flying snakes throw themselves from trees. They flatten their bodies to land safely.

The giant salamander can grow to be nearly 6 feet (1.8 m) long and breathes through its skin.

The Cantor's giant soft-shelled turtle takes just two breaths every day.

Glossary

adaptation: a change in a type of animal that makes it better able to live in its surroundings

census: the official process of counting the number of things and collecting information about them

crustacean: an animal with a hard shell, jointed limbs, feelers, and no backbone

descendant: an animal that comes from an animal of an earlier time

digest: to break down food inside the body so that the body can use it

estimate: to make a careful guess about an answer based on known facts

extinction: the death of all members of a species

gourmet: describing high-quality food

habitat: the natural place where an animal or plant lives

invertebrate: an animal that lacks a backbone

mollusk: an animal that lacks a backbone and has a soft body and usually a shell, such as a snail, clam, or octopus

pesticide: something used to kill pests, such as bugs that eat plants

porous: having small holes that allow air or water through

release: to set something free

sac: a part inside the body of an animal or plant that is shaped like a bag and that usually contains liquid or air

shed: to lose something as part of a normal process of life

snout: an animal's nose and mouth

species: a group of plants or animals that are all the same kind

talon: one of a bird's sharp claws

venom: something an animal makes in its body that can harm other animals

vitamin: a natural matter that is usually found in foods and that helps your body to be healthy

BOOKS

Loy, Jessica. *Weird & Wild Animal Facts*. New York, NY: Henry Holt and Company, 2015.

National Geographic Society. *Quiz Whiz: 1,000 Super Fun Mind-Bending Totally Awesome Trivia Questions*. Washington, DC: National Geographic, 2012.

Peterson, Megan Cooley. *This Book Might Bite: A Collection of Wacky Animal Trivia*. North Mankato, MN: Capstone Press, 2012.

WEBSITES

San Diego Zoo Kids: Meet the Animals
kids.sandiegozoo.org/animals
The spectacular San Diego Zoo offers a wealth of information about many kinds of animals.

Weird and Wild
news.nationalgeographic.com/weird-wild/
Check out this National Geographic site to find out the latest on weird and wild animals.

Index

Este  pertenece a

Para Xia y sus primos, grandes lectores. K. B.

Para Ron, a quien echo de menos. C. S.

Título original: THE LONELY BOOK

© del texto: Kate Bernheimer, 2012
© de las ilustraciones: Chris Sheban, 2012
Esta traducción ha sido publicada con el acuerdo
de Random House Children's Books, una división de Random House Inc.

Las ilustraciones se han realizado con acuarela,
grafito, y lápices de colores sobre papel.

© de la traducción castellana:
EDITORIAL JUVENTUD, S. A., 2012
Provença, 101 - 08029 Barcelona
info@editorialjuventud.es
www.editorialjuventud.es

Traducción de Teresa Farran

Primera edición, 2012
DL B 11960-2012
ISBN 978-84-261-3924-5
Núm. de edición de E. J.: 12.505

Printed in Spain
A.V.C. Gràfiques, Avda. Generalitat, 39 - Sant Joan Despí (Barcelona)

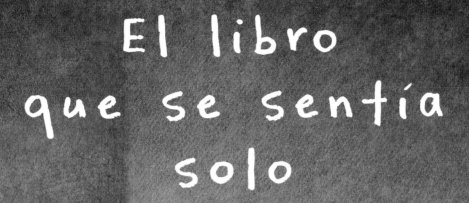

El libro
que se sentía
solo

Kate Bernheimer

Ilustraciones de
Chris Sheban

Editorial **EJ** Juventud

ÉRASE UNA VEZ un libro totalmente nuevo que llegó a la biblioteca. Era verde y llevaba una cinta amarilla para marcar las páginas. En la cubierta se veía a una niña debajo de una seta, en un bosque. El libro estaba en la entrada de la biblioteca, allí donde siempre se colocaban los libros nuevos.

La biblioteca siempre estaba muy concurrida, llena de niños que buscaban libros sobre cualquier cosa imaginable, y a menudo algún niño se llevaba a su casa aquel libro verde musgo de la niña en el bosque.

Cada vez que el libro era devuelto, volvían a colocarlo en el estante de los libros nuevos. Había una larga lista de espera de niños y niñas que querían llevarse el libro y raramente pasaba la noche en la biblioteca.

Como es habitual en las bibliotecas, después de un tiempo el libro fue trasladado a la sección infantil junto a otros libros muy bonitos que ya no eran nuevos. Pero todavía solían llevárselo y el libro todavía seguía siendo feliz.

Pasaron los años, y el libro ya solo salía en raras ocasiones. La cubierta estaba descolorida, en una página el vestido de parches marrones de la niña estaba rasgado, y faltaba la última página.

Pasaron todavía más años y ya casi nadie sacaba aquel viejo libro de la estantería. Pero de tanto en tanto algún niño o alguna niña lo leía y, a pesar de su aspecto desgastado, la historia de la niña y la seta seguía cautivando a sus lectores.

El libro empezó a sentirse solo.

Entonces, una tarde, el libro quedó completamente olvidado en un rincón, donde un pequeño lector despistado lo había dejado, y ni siquiera la bibliotecaria lo encontró.

A la mañana siguiente, una niña se sentó a leer en el rincón de la biblioteca donde dormía el pobre libro. Lo sintió debajo de la pata de la mecedora y se agachó y lo recogió. Al pasar las páginas, suspiró.

–¡Papá! –susurró, y atravesó la sección de cuentos–. Este es el libro más bonito que he leído. ¿Puedo llevármelo a casa?

–No lo sé, Alicia –contestó su padre inmerso en la lectura de un voluminoso libro tan grande como él mismo–. Parece muy delicado. Y ya tienes muchos libros en tu cesta.

Alicia devolvió tres libros nuevos y así pudo llevarse el libro solitario a su casa, prometiendo que tendría mucho cuidado con él.

Cuando el libro vio la habitación de Alicia y el estante donde iba a pasar la noche, junto a muchos libros que conocía de la biblioteca, y algunos nuevos que no había visto nunca, se puso muy contento.

Durante seis noches, el padre de Alicia le leyó el libro a la hora de dormir,

y cuando apagaba la luz,
ella lo seguía leyendo a la
luz de la luna.

Cuando llegaba a la última
página, la que faltaba, siempre
inventaba un final feliz con
unas hadas que bailaban con la
niña alrededor de la seta.

Alicia dormía con el libro
verde debajo de su almohada
para soñar con él.

Cada mañana a la hora de ir a la escuela, Alicia
metía cuidadosamente el libro dentro de su cartera.
Un día, el libro fue mostrado y leído en clase.

«Es de la biblioteca. Es un libro muy viejo sobre una niña y su vida debajo de una seta», dijo Alicia con orgullo.

El libro nunca se había sentido tan querido.

A la semana siguiente hubo un acontecimiento especial en la biblioteca. Una princesa y un león recibieron a Alicia y a todos los niños a su llegada y los condujeron a la Sala de Cuentos, donde les explicaron una maravillosa historia sobre una princesa y un león.

Al terminar el acto, Alicia escogió el cuento de la princesa y del león para llevárselo a casa. Con tantas emociones, se le olvidó por completo renovar el préstamo del viejo libro sobre la niña en el bosque.

Pero en cuanto Alicia llegó a casa, lo recordó.

—¡Papá! —exclamó—. Me he dejado el libro en la biblioteca. ¿Por favor, podemos volver para recogerlo?

—Lo siento, Alicia —contestó su padre—. La biblioteca ya está cerrada, y durante la semana tendré mucho trabajo, pero te prometo que te llevaré el próximo sábado por la mañana. Estoy seguro de que tu querido libro estará allí.

Al sábado siguiente, Alicia se precipitó hacia la sección infantil, pero el libro verde descolorido no estaba allí. La bibliotecaria buscó y volvió a buscar, pero tampoco lo encontró. (Un afanoso voluntario de la biblioteca lo había recogido y, creyendo que estaba destinado a la venta, lo había bajado al sótano. Allí el libro solitario esperaba pacientemente que ocurriera algo.)

Alicia encontró muchos otros libros para llevarse a casa, pero ninguno se le parecía. Cada sábado buscaba su libro, pero nunca estaba. Alicia lo echaba mucho de menos.

Y el libro solitario echaba de menos a Alicia. Aunque los libros estuvieran bien cuidados en el sótano, el lugar era muy oscuro. El libro se sentía más solo que nunca.

Con el tiempo, Alicia se olvidó del libro. Si bien nunca dejó de quererlo, en su cabeza fue sustituido por otros: uno, particularmente bonito, acerca de un caballito de mar y su casa submarina, y otro misterioso sobre el hielo, la nieve y el cristal.

Mientras tanto, en la biblioteca los voluntarios bajaban de vez en cuando al sótano para ocuparse de los libros o llevarles nuevos compañeros. A veces un voluntario cogía el libro solitario, lo hojeaba y sonreía al recordar la seta maravillosa. Pero siempre volvía a dejarlo con un suspiro y se iba.

El libro se sentía cada vez más solo.

Y entonces llegó un día que el libro no olvidaría jamás. Una mañana lo llevaron escaleras arriba y lo colocaron a la sombra de un árbol.

El libro disfrutaba del aire fresco. Durante todo el día, pasó gente que lo miraba con simpatía, y muchos niños lo cogían y lo hojeaban. Algunos se llevaban otros libros bajo el brazo, libros fantásticos sobre toda clase de temas, como planetas lejanos o perros habladores. Aun así, ninguno era tan mágico como el libro solitario. Tampoco ninguno estaba tan estropeado, y tal vez por eso nadie se lo llevaba.

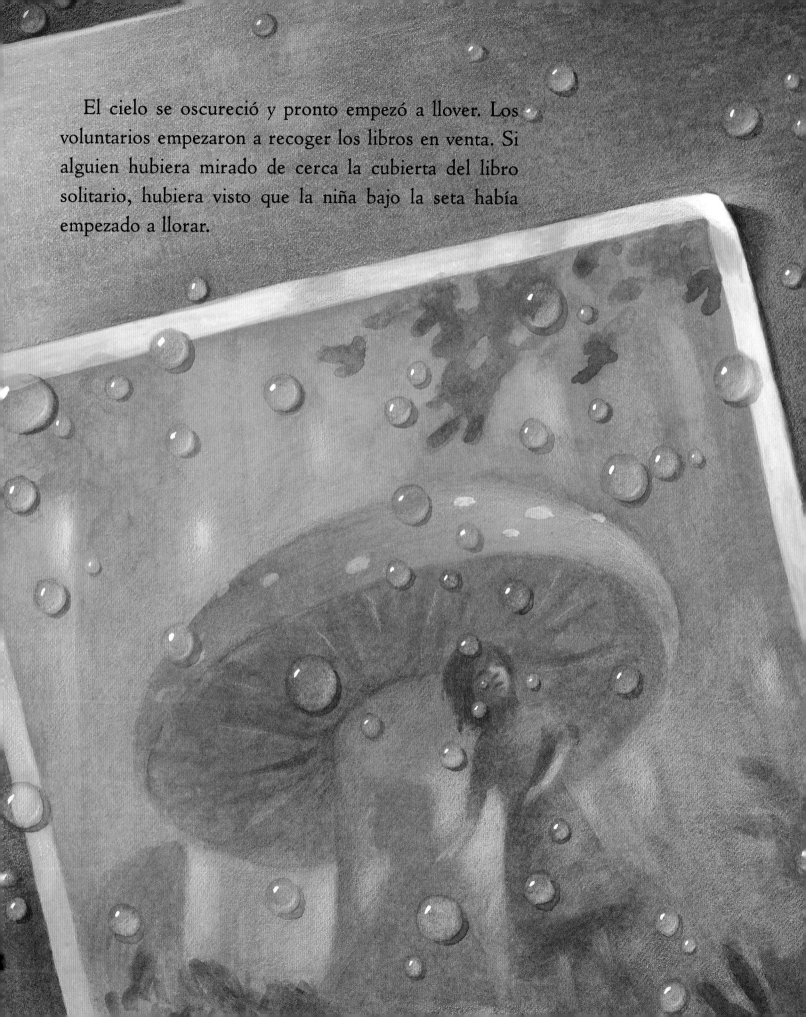

El cielo se oscureció y pronto empezó a llover. Los voluntarios empezaron a recoger los libros en venta. Si alguien hubiera mirado de cerca la cubierta del libro solitario, hubiera visto que la niña bajo la seta había empezado a llorar.

Poco después, el libro oyó una voz familiar.

—Sé que está aquí, estoy segura. Me daré prisa, lo prometo —dijo una voz entrecortada a la bibliotecaria.

—De acuerdo, cariño, porque tenemos que recoger los libros para que no se mojen —contestó la bibliotecaria.

Y entonces... el libro se encontró de nuevo entre las manos de Alicia.

—¡Sabía que te encontraría! —exclamó Alicia, acariciando la desgastada cinta amarilla.

—¡Oh, Alicia, confiaba en que vinieras! —dijo la bibliotecaria—. El libro estaba esperándote. Llévatelo, es un regalo.

»Sabes —añadió, echando una mirada a la cubierta del libro con la niña y la seta encantada—, también era mi libro favorito cuando era pequeña.

De vuelta a la habitación de Alicia, el libro se sintió feliz de encontrarse por fin en la que sería su casa para siempre. Alicia arregló el vestido rasgado de la niña con cinta adhesiva y leyó la historia en voz alta.

–No me importa nada que falte esta página –dijo al llegar a la última–. Sé lo que pone: «Y vivieron felices para siempre», naturalmente.